YOUTH ENCLOSED

HANDLE WITH CARE

Lillenas® Drama

THREE ONE-ACT PLAYS FOR TEENS

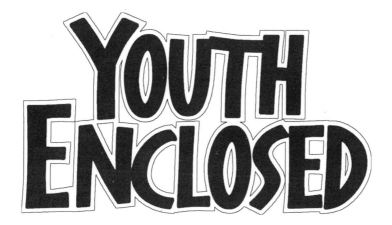

YOUTH ENCLOSED

HANDLE WITH CARE

BY JERRY COHAGAN, BOB HOOSE, & JIM CUSTER

Lillenas® PUBLISHING COMPANY

KANSAS CITY, MO 64141

CONTENTS

FIFTH HOUR

by
Jerry Cohagan

Setting:

The action takes place in two areas. There is the hallway of a typical suburban high school, stage left, lined with lockers upstage. There is a bench in the hallway against the wall, which divides the two playing areas. Next to the bench is a door leading to Ms. Bennett's classroom, stage right. Her desk is upstage just inside the door, and there are several rows of desk chairs running parallel to the back wall, which has several windows.

Characters:

MS. BENNETT: *Ms. Bennett is a high school English teacher. She is an attractive, intelligent woman in her early 30s. She has a good sense of humor and genuinely cares for her students.*

ALYSON: *She is a senior high school student. She is also a knockout and knows it. She always has a crowd around her.*

MONICA: *She is also a senior. She is always on the fringes of Alyson's crowd. She is very smart and is almost apologetic for it. She is nice-looking, but withdrawn.*

DEREK: *He is a senior high school student who lives for his car. He is good-looking and a bit brash. His MO is to appear cocksure and untouchable. He is also empty inside.*

WESLEY: *Called "Weazer," he is a nice guy who is always good for a laugh. A senior as well, he is not so much looking to fit in as just making sure he doesn't stand out. Wants badly to be Derek's friend.*

STUDENT 1: *Female student, part of Alyson's crowd.*

STUDENT 2: *Female student, part of Alyson's crowd.*

STUDENT 3: *Male student.*

STUDENT 4: *Male student, athletic, wears a leather school jacket.*

STUDENT 5: *Female student, parents divorced, lives with her mother.*

JANITOR: *Male in his 50s.*

EXTRAS: *Various extras can be used to fill out the classroom and hall.*

Props:

MS. BENNETT: A briefcase

ALYSON: Several pages of notes on notebook paper

MONICA: Several schoolbooks and various supplies

DEREK: Keys with remote car lock button that beeps, cellular phone, car wax and cloth

STUDENT 4: A typical school leather jacket

Paperback copies of *The Scarlet Letter* for each student, along with various school supplies.

(At rise, lights come up to reveal the hallway and classroom. Everything looks new and unused. The lockers look spotless, the bench is empty. The desks in the classroom are all neatly aligned, and the teacher's desk has nothing on it. It is a beginning. After a moment a voice is heard.)

Ms. BENNETT *(offstage left):* The first day of school. I always dread it. I get sweaty palms, my stomach is full of butterflies, and my knees feel like Jell-O. And there are always a thousand questions running through my head. What should I wear? Will I make new friends? What if I say something really stupid? What'll my classes be like?

(Ms. BENNETT walks onstage in the hallway carrying a briefcase. She is an attractive woman in her early 30s.)

Ms. BENNETT *(addressing the audience, smiles):* I'm sure the students are nervous too. No matter how many years I teach, I still fear the first day. How will I come across to my students? Will they see Hitler in heels or Mother Teresa instead? *(Smiles)* Probably a little bit of both. *(Crosses to her classroom and enters; lights fade out in the hall.)* It's hard to represent authority and still be a friend. I'm not even sure it's possible. *(Crosses to her desk and places briefcase on it)* So, which face will I wear this year? I guess in that respect, there's not that much difference between us and them. *(Opens briefcase and begins readying her desk)* Kids are always trying to find out who they are, where they fit in, trying on different faces, striking attitudes, seeing which one works best for them. All the time trying to keep their guard up. Some parents seem to have forgotten what it was like. They just throw their hands up in the air, shrug their shoulders, and thank the Lord that summer's finally over. It's not that we don't understand our kids, it's just that we'd rather not remember when we were that age. It's easier to shake our heads and just give it a name. *(Smiling)* We call it adolescence. But I'm not sure any of us ever outgrow it. Maybe it's just the first sure sign of adulthood. *(Wanders among desks and makes her way downstage)* But I'll never forget my fifth hour last year. They were typical of most of my senior classes; some there to learn, some there to kill an English credit, some there just to kill time. But one cloudy, gray day last spring something unusual happened. And for a few moments, we all forgot where we were and who we were trying to be. You see, briefly, we let our guard down. *(Turns and crosses back to her desk as thunder is heard gently rumbling in the distance, then a bell sounds indicating a change of class.)*

(Lights up full in hallway to reveal typical school day. There is lots of activity. Students are passing through the hall. Several students are at their lockers, including ALYSON. MONICA is seated on the bench, studying.)

STUDENT 1: So, Alyson, how many times has he asked you out this month?

ALYSON *(she's a looker, and knows it):* Counting this weekend . . . 10.

STUDENT 2: No kidding? And how many times have you turned him down?

ALYSON (closes her locker and stares at her friends): Twelve . . .

(They all look at each other knowingly and laugh, ALYSON just smiles icily and crosses to MONICA. The group follows on her heels.)

STUDENT 1: How could you? He's got such a cool car.

ALYSON: Yeah, but that's all he's got. (Handing MONICA several sheets of notes) Monica, I can't read this. Your handwriting is horrible. I need you to recopy it before the test tomorrow.

MONICA (taking notes): Sorry. I'll give it to you after school.

ALYSON: I mean, how am I supposed to pass if I can't read your handwriting?

(ALYSON and friends cross on into classroom, chatting as they go. DEREK and STUDENT 3 enter stage left.)

STUDENT 3: Hey, Derek, how 'bout a ride home after class?

DEREK: No can do.

STUDENT 3: Why? I'm on your way.

DEREK: It might be raining.

STUDENT: I know, that's why I want the ride.

DEREK: And that's exactly why I can't give you a ride. You got any idea what water does to a leather interior?

STUDENT 3 (holding his hands up in surrender): Hey, whatever . . . (Crossing to classroom) Cool car, though.

(DEREK casually points his remote car/lock key chain stage left behind his back and beeps it.)

DEREK: Yeah, I know . . .

(STUDENT 3 heads on into class while DEREK crosses to his locker. He pulls out a small cellular phone from inside his coat pocket, flips it open, and punches in a number. WESLEY enters and crosses to DEREK and tries to appear casual. He leans on DEREK's locker.)

WESLEY: Hey, Derek.

DEREK (staring hard at WESLEY): Weazer, what are you doing?

WESLEY: What? (Notices his faux pas and straightens up) Oh, sorry.

(Getting no answer, DEREK flips shut his cellular phone, tosses it in his locker, and pulls out a can of Turtle Wax and a cloth. He tosses them to WESLEY.)

DEREK: Remember, small circles. Not up and down. (Starts to cross to classroom)

WESLEY: Right. *(Runs after him)* So, how was your weekend?

DEREK: What's it to you?

WESLEY *(genuinely sympathetic, just trying too hard)*: Struck out again, huh? What's that make, 10 in a row? Boy, what that must do to your self-esteem. You must really feel like a loser.

DEREK *(taking the obvious cheap shot)*: I don't know. What's it feel like?

WESLEY *(trying to make a joke)*: If I tell ya, we got something in common, right?

(DEREK stares at him, then starts off again.)

WESLEY *(stopping him again)*: Why do you keep asking her out?

DEREK *(looking in the class at ALYSON)*: 'Cause she's perfect. On a scale of 1 to 10, she's a 20.

WESLEY: Yeah, but she's got a wind chill factor of minus 50.

(WESLEY watches as DEREK catches ALYSON's eye and suavely nods in her direction. ALYSON eyes DEREK briefly, then turns away. She is ice.)

WESLEY: Man, that's one cold refrigerator.

DEREK: Yeah, but it's so well-stocked.

(MONICA rises from bench and crosses in front of DEREK and WESLEY, heading into the classroom.)

MONICA *(trying not to be noticed)*: Excuse me.

(They fall in behind her, entering the classroom.)

WESLEY *(teasing her)*: I'll take "Brains" for a thousand, Alex.

DEREK: And the answer is, "The only person to throw off the curve on every test ever given."

(DEREK and WESLEY hum the "Jeopardy" theme while circling MONICA.)

WESLEY: Who is Monica Pelt?

DEREK: Correct! *(They high-five each other while MONICA slides into her desk.)*

WESLEY *(to MONICA)*: If it wasn't for you, I'd be a straight C student.

DEREK: In your dreams, Weazer. *(Heads toward his desk)*

WESLEY *(following him, still carrying cloth and wax)*: Hey, wait. Which side am I doing?

DEREK: What is today?

WESLEY: Monday . . . ?

DEREK (*as if to a child*): That's right. Monday is the left side, Tuesday is the right, Wednesday is the hood, and Thursday is the trunk. (*Puts an arm around* WESLEY *and leads him over to his own desk*) And what's Friday?

WESLEY: Touch-up.

DEREK (*hands him a buck, speaks a bit louder so the entire class can share in his wit*): Verrrry goooood. Weazer, how are you ever gonna make head fryboy if you can't remember anything?

(DEREK *crosses over to his own desk shaking his head.* WESLEY *is embarrassed as a couple students snicker at him.*)

WESLEY (*to* DEREK's *back*): See you after class.

(DEREK *doesn't even look back, just waves him off and slumps into his desk.* WESLEY *looks at* DEREK *for a moment, then notices his hands are full with the cloth and wax, and sits at his desk. A bell sounds somewhere in the building, indicating class has begun. Several more students find their seats while* MS. BENNETT *finishes shuffling a few papers at her desk.*)

MS. BENNETT (*rises and crosses to front of classroom*): All right, everyone, let's find our seats. I hope everybody found some time this weekend to continue reading *The Scarlet Letter*. (*Several moans from students*) Ah, the sound of young minds eager to learn. . . . Come on, who can get us started today? (*She looks around the class for a volunteer. None is forthcoming. Her eyes finally come to rest on* WESLEY, *who has his head buried as low as possible.*) Wesley, how about you? Can you bring us up to date?

WESLEY (*slowly sitting up*): Well, I'll try. (*Resorting to buffoonery*) I believe it's April 5.

MS. BENNETT: Wonderful, now that we all know you can read a calendar, how about the book?

WESLEY (*nailed again*): Seriously, I meant to read it, Ms. Bennett. But I just got too busy.

DEREK (*speaking up for the benefit of the entire class*): Things really hoppin' at the drive-through window, huh, Weazer?

(*A couple of snickers,* WESLEY *joins in at his own expense.*)

ALYSON (*directing her comment toward* DEREK, *but not looking at him*): I'm sure you must know. It must be tough ordering a *single* every Friday night. (*Several students acknowledge the direct hit.*)

MS. BENNETT: All right, that's enough about your social lives. Let's get back to the subject at hand. (*Crosses back to her desk and leans on the front of it*) As you may or may not recall, Hester Prynne has been found guilty of adultery. As punishment she has been sentenced to wear the letter *A* on the front of her clothing whenever she appears in public. (*Moving about the classroom)* And what about the Rev. Arthur Dimmesdale? The community perceives him as a very pious, holy man. But is he? *(No response is forthcoming; thunder rumbles in the distance.)* . . . Monica?

MONICA *(hating the fact that she's been called on, she looks around apologetically, then answers correctly, as usual):* No. He appears to the public as a righteous man. But we, the readers, know that he's the one who committed adultery with Hester. And because of his hypocrisy, he is guilt-ridden. Yet he can't bring himself to confess his guilt. His sin, besides adultery, is trying to be something he is not.

MS. BENNETT: That's right—

DEREK *(under his breath, but loud enough to be heard):* Wow, there's a shock. *(To* MONICA*)* You sound like walking Cliff Notes.

MS. BENNETT: Well, Derek. You seem eager to comment. *(Crossing back to her desk)* Why don't you come on up and start reading where we left off last Friday.

DEREK *(muttering under his breath):* Great . . . *(Walks to the front of the class, begins thumbing through his book)* I seem to have lost my place. Where exactly are we?

MS. BENNETT: Page 250 . . .

DEREK: Ah, got it . . . *(Creases back the page)* Book seems a little stiff.

MS. BENNETT *(with irony):* That'll happen when it's never been opened. Anytime, Derek . . .

(DEREK clears his throat and just as he is about to actually start reading a loud flash of lightning is heard and seen through the windows. The lights in the classroom suddenly flash off and on a couple of times and then go out entirely. In the darkness the thunder rumbles, then dies out.)

DEREK *(beat, then glances heavenward):* Thank You, God. *(Closes book and sits back at desk)*

(There is general chatter among the students. The stage is semidark except for the gray light that comes from outside through the windows upstage. It is just enough to make out everyone and reflects the oncoming storm outside.)

MS. BENNETT: All right, everyone just stay seated. I'm sure they'll be back on in a minute.

(MS. BENNETT crosses to door and steps out into hall as JANITOR hurries by.)

MS. BENNETT: What happened?

JANITOR: Looks like a circuit breaker blew.

MS. BENNETT: How long until it's fixed?

JANITOR: Don't know. With this coming storm, could be awhile. *(Hurries on down the hall)*

(Ms. BENNETT crosses back into her classroom. As she enters several students hold up Bic lighters.)

STUDENT 3: Need a light, Ms. Bennett?

STUDENT 1: My dad said this would happen if they kept cutting the school budget.

Ms. BENNETT *(smiling good-naturedly):* It's not that dark in here. Put the lighters away. Until the lights come back on, we can't very well read. *(Several mock groans are heard while a couple of students high-five each other.)* I know it breaks your hearts. So, instead of reading the book, let's talk about it. *(The mock groans turn real.)* Once again, music to my ears.

DEREK: Talk about it?

Ms. BENNETT: Yes. Talk about it.

STUDENT 2: You mean like on *Oprah?*

Ms. BENNETT: Yes, like on *Oprah.* You know, discuss the book. Is it relevant to us today?

STUDENT 4: You mean the adultery part?

(Several snickers from the class)

Ms. BENNETT: No, I mean the letter part. The townspeople only saw Hester wearing that big, scarlet *A.* They couldn't see beyond that. *(Points to STUDENT 4's school leather jacket)* What letters do we wear? Do we see each other only as a certain letter? Do we allow one another to deviate from the letter we assign them?

ALYSON: What do you mean?

Ms. BENNETT: Well, how do you all perceive me? Am I just the letter *T* to you? Or do you see beyond the "teacher"?

DEREK: I'm just trying to "see" my way to lunch.

Ms. BENNETT *(addressing the whole class):* Did you know I have a 13-year-old son?

STUDENT 3: You don't seem that old.

Ms. BENNETT: I'm 30.

STUDENT 1: But I thought you were single?

Ms. BENNETT: I am.

STUDENT 5 *(explaining it to* MS. BENNETT*)*: That means that you're not married.

MS. BENNETT: No, but I was. I've been divorced for 10 years.

MONICA *(figuring it out):* Wait a minute. If you're 30, that means you would've been in high school when you had your—(MONICA *stops abruptly as realization dawns.)*

(An awkward moment of silence while students figure it out and glance around. We can just make out the sound of faint thunder rumbling in the distance.)

MS. BENNETT: Now I know how Hester Prynne felt.

DEREK *(to* MONICA*)*: Way to go, Monica. Math skills, 100. Tact, zero.

STUDENT 5: No, it's not that. It's just that my parents got a divorce three years ago. My mom still seems so unhappy, and you seem to have it all together . . . *(Looks around a bit self-consciously, dismisses it)* Never mind.

MS. BENNETT: No, that's all right. It hasn't been easy being a single parent. And if I could go back and do some things over, I'd make smarter choices. *(To the whole class)* But what about you? You're all making choices now, just like I did, that are going to affect who you are for the rest of your life. If you could pick a letter that represented you, what would it be? How do you think people perceive you?

STUDENT 4: That's easy. *J* for jock. Funny thing is, I don't like sports that much.

(Various students ad-lib "yeah, right," "I'm sure," etc.)

MS. BENNETT *(to class):* Let's let him talk. Go on.

STUDENT 4 *(standing up):* No, I mean it. It's just something I can do. My dad doesn't miss a game. He loves to watch me play. Actually, he loves to watch me win. At first, that's why I did it—to win. It made him proud of me. But anymore, I don't know . . . I think I do it now 'cause I'm scared to quit. *(Sits back down)*

DEREK *(after a moment, sarcastic):* Right. You don't like sports like Weazer doesn't have zits. *(Sniggers)*

MONICA *(firing off at* DEREK*)*: Or like you don't get turned down by Alyson.

DEREK *(firing back):* Or like you don't have more brain matter than personality.

MS. BENNETT: That's enough, Derek.

MONICA *(speaking over* MS. BENNETT; *rises facing* DEREK*)*: That's right. I don't mind being smart. *(Realizes what she's just said, after a moment continues to the whole class)* My sister was at the top of her class and so was my brother. I guess brain matter just runs in our family.

DEREK *(backing off a bit):* A genetic brain pool.

16

MONICA: At least I'm not at the shallow end. *(To the whole class)* I've heard 'em all, you know. "Einstein's little sister." If I were a Chinese restaurant, I'd be high I.Q.—

STUDENT 2 *(referring to joke):* Oh, that's lame.

MONICA: It was OK when I was smart in elementary school. But somewhere in junior high, it was no longer cool for girls to be smart. While you guys read *Outdoor Life* and *Computer World* I was supposed to be reading *Seventeen* and hanging posters of Luke Perry in my room. I mean, face it. Magazines for guys teach you how to be smart, and magazines for girls teach us how to be thin and apply eye shadow. Well, I made a choice. I could either be myself and not have many friends, or I could dummy down to get a social life.

WEAZER *(referring to himself):* Hey, being dumb doesn't guarantee a social life.

MONICA: Maybe not. But acing your PSAT's doesn't exactly get your phone ringing on a Friday night either.

Ms. BENNETT *(to* MONICA*):* Why do you copy your notes for Alyson?

*(*ALYSON *looks over at* MONICA, *mortified.)*

MONICA *(stunned as well, to* ALYSON*):* I never told her . . . !

Ms. BENNETT *(eerily, but smiling):* I see and know all. *(Beat, then)* Why do you do it?

MONICA *(searching for a way out):* I don't know, I just do . . . I don't mind. I figure if it helps her get better grades, then great.

STUDENT 3: You don't feel used?

MONICA *(justifying):* No . . . Well, maybe some, yeah . . . *(Referring to* ALYSON*)* But we're friends. Look, maybe we don't do much together. But that's just because I study so much. It's not that Alyson uses me. Really, it isn't . . . *(*MONICA *looks over at* ALYSON, *who is sitting rigidly in her desk staring straight ahead. Looking back to the class.)* . . . It's my choice. *(Slowly sits back down; faint thunder is heard in the distance.)*

Ms. BENNETT *(to* ALYSON*):* Why don't you take your own notes, Alyson? . . . Alyson?

ALYSON *(mortified that she has to explain herself, she continues to stare straight ahead):* I have to go to one of two colleges next year. Either Penn State or UCLA. It's important to me that I get accepted to one of those two.

Ms. BENNETT: That's why you have Monica copy all her notes for you?

ALYSON *(turning to* Ms. BENNETT*):* Is that so terrible? It's not like I'm cheating. I'm just not that good at studying, you know. *(Looks around for support)*

Look, I'm not all that smart, OK? Is that what you want to hear? School-work doesn't come easy for me like it does for some. *(Honestly)* I mean, what if I'm not college material?

DEREK *(seriously):* Is that so bad?

MS. BENNETT: Have you thought about a junior college for a couple of years, to find out? Or do you just expect to find another Monica wherever you go?

ALYSON: You don't understand, I've got to go to a name school. Or at least one on the coast. That's important to me. I want to be involved in a good soror-ity. And even some of *them* have grade point qualifications. *(A bit desper-ate)* If I don't go to a name school—I mean, what'll people think of me?

MS. BENNETT: What people think of you isn't based on what college you go to or what sorority you join. It's based on who you really are, your personality.

ALYSON *(missing the irony):* That is *so* unfair.

WESLEY *(shaking his head, smiling):* Ms. Bennett, don't take this wrong, but I don't even want to be an A student.

DEREK: Nothing to worry about there, Weazer . . .

WESLEY: And as far as my I.Q. goes, I just wanna be above sea level.

DEREK: Quick! Somebody throw him a life jacket! *(A couple of snickers)*

WESLEY *(ignoring DEREK):* I mean, someone like me and her . . . *(referring to ALYSON)* We move in two entirely different stratospheres. My high school counselor's always throwing the *P* word at me. "You're not living up to your 'potential.' Don't you want to realize your 'potential'?" Well, to be honest . . . I guess I don't. I've always wanted to say to him, "Look, if *you* were living up to *your* potential, you wouldn't still be in high school either!" *(Several students chuckle)* I just want to fit in . . . You know, be an average joe.

DEREK: Trust me, Weazer. You have realized your potential.

MS. BENNETT *(to DEREK):* And what about you? You seem to have plenty to say about everyone else. Who are you?

DEREK: You want to know who I am, look at my car.

ALYSON *(with an attitude):* You're your car?

STUDENT 1 *(looking DEREK over):* Nice bumper . . .

DEREK *(to ALYSON):* Look, everybody's gotta have a hobby. You're into mousse—I'm into my car.

MS. BENNETT: That seems kind of empty, Derek.

DEREK: Uh-oh, I feel the *P* word coming on. Ms. Bennett, I'm not into all this in-trospective, self-examination stuff.

Ms. Bennett *(gently):* That's too bad. It's one examination you might pass.

Derek *(rises):* Look, everybody here's trying to be something they're not. *(Referring to* Alyson*)* Miss Deep Freeze is scared to death to be anything but popular. *(Pointing to* Student 4*)* He's trying to live up to his dad's expectations. *(To* Monica*)* Miss Cerebellum is trying to convince herself that she's not being used, and Weazer's an idiot. I mean, what's the point?

Ms. Bennett: The point is that every once in awhile it's good to see who we really are, not what we want people to think we are. It's important to be able to look at yourself, and to like what you see.

Derek *(beat, then slumps back in his chair):* Yeah? Well, I'm my car . . .

Wesley *(to* Derek*)*: I'm not as dumb as I act, you know.

Derek: Yes, you are.

Wesley: No, I'm not.

Derek *(as if to a simpleton):* Yes, you are.

Wesley *(rising):* No, I'm not. I just don't want to be treated the same way we all treat her. *(Referring to* Monica*)* Being smart doesn't look like much fun. You may find this hard to believe, Ms. Bennett, but I've been reading the book. *(Some general heckling from a couple students "Oh, right," "Sure you have, Weazer"; faint thunder heard)* And I even like it. But telling all of you that doesn't win me any friends.

Ms. Bennett: What do you like best about it, Wesley?

Derek *(mocking him):* That's right, *Wesley.* Share with us your favorite passage. But then, lucky for you, it's too dark to read.

Wesley: That's OK. I don't need the light. *(Heckling slowly subsides as* Wesley *steps forward and faces the class. He recites from memory.)* "No man, for any considerable period, can wear one face to himself, and another to the multitude, without finally getting bewildered as to which may be the true."

(Students all stare at Wesley *in various degrees of mild shock. After a moment he slowly smiles at them as thunder begins to rumble in the distance growing louder. The remaining light fades.*

(After several moments of darkness, the thunder fades out. A pool of light falls on Ms. Bennett *at her desk. The room is empty, and her briefcase is open on her desk as at the beginning.)*

Ms. Bennett *(addressing the audience):* And that's when I realized something unique was beginning to happen. Slowly, as some of the students began to open up, I no longer saw just the letter *S* around their necks. I wasn't just teaching anymore, I was listening. I don't know . . . maybe it was just dark enough that they felt safe and anonymous. No one's lives were changed in those few minutes. But maybe their perspective of each other was, just a little. Maybe they began to see more than just the face each student tried to carry in front of them all year. And maybe for one or two students who lowered their mask, they began to like what they saw . . . (Continues to unpack her briefcase)

(Lights come up in the hallway. MONICA is seated on the bench, copying her notes. WESLEY is leaning on DEREK's locker with the wax and cloth in his hands. DEREK enters from stage left and crosses to him.)

DEREK: I thought I made it clear to do the left side.

WESLEY (throwing him the cloth): I can't do this anymore. It's not worth it.

DEREK: Fine . . . I can find somebody else during study hall. You're not the only loser in the school. (Opens his locker and starts to toss cloth in it, then stops) Hey, Weazer? I thought you needed this? (Referring to the cloth and himself)

WESLEY: No, Derek. I needed the friendship. (Holds up the car wax) This . . . has no "potential." (WESLEY tosses it to DEREK, turns and saunters off stage left.)

Ms. BENNETT (to the audience): By the end of the year, Monica wasn't the only one throwing off the curve. (Smiling) It seemed Wesley no longer feared the P word.

(DEREK shrugs and turns back to his locker, pulls out the cellular phone, and places call again.)

DEREK (after a moment, excited): Hey, Dad, it's me. Yeah, I got it. I'm calling you on it! It works great. So, what time Friday will you get here—? (DEREK waits, then.) You said that last week— (Listens, dejected) Yeah . . . Yeah, I know . . . (Dad is obviously trying to change the subject. DEREK closes his eyes.) No, the car's great. I love it, Dad . . . Oh yeah, lot's of dates. (DEREK turns slightly into his locker door.) Dad, listen. It's been almost a year . . . (Pleading softly) I know, but I need to see you— (DEREK listens, then gives up.) Yeah, sure . . . no, I'll call . . . every day. It's not the same though, Dad. (DEREK's last hope.) What about graduation? . . . Yeah . . . (He's heard all these excuses before. He is genuinely hurt.) OK, we'll see . . . No, I know . . . I will . . . Me too . . . Bye. (Looks briefly at phone, then tosses it in locker and shuts door and turns to see MONICA looking at him. She has obviously heard this one-sided conversation. He is caught with his guard down. After a moment of indecision he starts to risk it.) That was my dad. Great guy, he's just, uh, I don't know . . . (DEREK's voice falters a bit.) Sometimes he . . .

(As DEREK is about to open up ALYSON and her group enter stage left, talking among themselves. She crosses to her locker.)

ALYSON (not even looking in MONICA's direction): I need those notes, Monica.

MONICA (crossing to ALYSON, almost apologetic): Here they are. I recopied them.

ALYSON (looking them over): Great. This is much better.

MS. BENNETT: Alyson graduated that spring. And, although it wasn't the coast, she was accepted at Penn State.

(MONICA crosses back to bench and sits. She watches DEREK, who has his head down.)

MS. BENNETT (continues): Monica went to college, as well. She went to the coast. Stanford on a full scholarship.

(ALYSON and group start to leave. DEREK steps in front of her, trying to recover some of his swagger, and starts to put the moves on her.)

DEREK (dangling his keys in front of her): What do ya say, Alyson? Just around the block. You can even drive!

(ALYSON, enjoying it, gives him the Frigidaire treatment. She steps around him and exits with her entourage. DEREK, a bit lost, turns and looks at MONICA. They look at each other for a moment.)

MS. BENNETT: Derek graduated as well but didn't go to college. He can be seen pretty much every Friday night driving around in his car.

(After a moment, DEREK smiles a bit dismissively and turns away and follows after ALYSON, exiting stage left. MONICA looks off stage left, then resumes her studying. Lights in the hall slowly begin to fade to a dim spot on MONICA at the bench during the following.)

MS. BENNETT (continuing): I wonder what this year will hold. But I know that last year, for a few brief moments on a cloudy, gray day it was just dark enough to share a bit of ourselves. Maybe Hawthorne said it best (opens book and reads): "So they lingered an instant longer. No golden light had ever been so precious as the gloom of this dark forest."

(Pool of light fades on MS. BENNETT as she closes book. After a moment the remaining light fades out on MONICA.)

BEFORE CLASS AND AFTER

by
Bob Hoose

Setting:

The play's action all takes place in the same classroom. The scenes are designed to overlap each other, representing different incidental moments of time in the 60-year life span of this school in rural America. The play's pacing should proceed briskly but with a life of its own based on the mood of a given scene. Characters in scenes that briefly overlap one another should of course ignore anyone not in their own scene.

Characters (in order of appearance):

ALICE: *Her time is the mid-1930s. She should be dressed in flowing skirts and starched shirt with a bow in her hair. Sweet and sincere.*

JOANNE: *Another 1930s girl. A bit of a follower. Sincere, but feels she is somewhat worldly-wise.*

MARY: *1930s attire. Somewhat forward and boy hungry but still a product of her time.*

SUE: *She and her friend Lynn both are typical 1950 stereotypes. Soft, furry sweaters, knee-length flair skirts, adorned perhaps with a poodle or two, hair pulled up in a ponytail. She is perky to the max.*

LYNN: *Dutiful friend, perhaps a bit heavier than Sue, but modeling herself after her best friend.*

RAZZ: *Total grunge in attitude and dress. From her wild hair to her multiple nose piercings she's a girl who embodies the dichotomy of being in the "in crowd" but with the external attitude of "who gives a rip?"*

CHEZ: *See above. Ditto. Whatever.*

HAROLD: *A 1960s nice guy. Plays on the baseball team. Average student. Solid, consistent.*

BETH: *A very pretty, soft, relaxed girl who just hasn't ever had a good record with boyfriends. She always picks the wrong types.*

TED: *Definite '70s stereotype greaseball. He's not too aggressive, not too much of anything really. He is just trying to be mellow. He's got one sore spot, though. Very '70s unwashed.*

ROY: *A '70s unhip throwback that never really understood the hippie hype. He's tried to figure things out in his own way, though, so he's pretty level-headed. Not a person to be outspoken but certainly has a well-formed set of beliefs.*

NICK: *A modern-day wallflower type. He's someone you'd miss in a crowd. A nervous worrying type.*

PETE: *An average nice guy who's just a little confused about his role in the world. He wants to be a world beater but just not sure of the path.*

JOE: *Confident jock. Not too smart but energetic. Good friend with Pete and very willing to support Pete's guest.*

LINK: *Definite dim bulb. Sort of a West Coast throwback.*

JULIE: *Very aggressive '90s woman. She is very sure of herself, dresses in jeans and sweatshirt, sharp, attractive, but not afraid of her tomboyish qualities. Thinks Pete and his gang are funny in light of their naive choices. Pete's friend, but he'd like it to be more and she knows it.*

MRS. CLERMONT: *60 plus in age. She's been at this school pretty much since the beginning. She understands its pulse and its new growths. She's also saddened by her retirement and the loss of the young people she's nurtured and loved for so many years. Has she really made a difference with all her years of efforts and prayers?*

ANITA: *A sweet, quiet girl. Probably with a less-than-privileged homelife. An almost sad-looking but still confident young lady. She's not tough, but she is strong.*

MICK: *Stereotypical, thickheaded, jock type. Not very concerned with anything outside the gym at school. Anxious to get on with summer break.*

Props:

The costumes in this play need to be elaborate enough to help support the given time period that the characters are supposed to be a part of. The props, however, can be minimal. A few papers and books, a Bible, an occasional backpack, and a class bell are all that's needed.

(At rise, the play opens in a typical classroom. The upstage wall is filled with windows through which we see a gently sloping grassed area with an occasional tree or swing set. The remaining walls may be composed of a blackboard and one or two "math" charts showing multiplication tables or some other appropriate math applications. A teacher's desk and several student desks are placed in the playing area to give the impression of a class filled with desks and chairs but leaving a majority of the playing space open for easy movement. As the lights come up, a young girl tentatively enters followed by two friends. All three girls are dressed in demure 1930s style apparel.)

ALICE *(walks to the window and looks out. She turns back thoughtfully and smiles):* Isn't it beautiful? Why, it's simply enormous. And this is only one classroom. Can you imagine?

JOANNE: It's certainly big. I for one, though, feel it loses the warmth of the old schoolhouse.

MARY: I agree. Why, you could probably go all day without seeing a single upperclassman in a school this large.

ALICE: Oh, piffle. The only reason you want to stay cramped in that little old schoolhouse is so you can moon over Henry Clermont all day. *(Rapturously)* Oh, Henry!

MARY: Now you stop that, Alice. I've not been mooning over Henry. He's just a nice young man who happens to show me his attentions. I was simply concerned that in this school, we might not receive the proper interaction with all grade levels.

JOANNE: I'm sure it has nothing to do with the fact that Stephanie Miller will be in all of Henry's classes and you can't keep an eye on either of them.

MARY: Of course not. Now don't you start too. I really couldn't care less. (JOANNE *laughs.)*

ALICE: Well, I think all the upperclassmen are perfectly Neanderthal, especially Henry. You can keep him.

MARY: Hmph. *(She walks to the window, disgruntled.)*

ALICE: But I'll keep this school. It's truly wonderful. *(She spins herself around, enjoying the space.)* Just think of the hundreds, maybe thousands, who will walk these halls over the next hundred years. *(She slides in behind a desk.)* They'll sit behind these desks and begin their lives, just like us, right here. Dreaming dreams of the future. Isn't it wonderful to be the first ones. *(She runs her hands over the smooth desktop.)* The first to dream.

MARY: Alice, you're such a romantic. The only thing of value this school has to offer is an indoor privy. However, I still find it very difficult to get mushy about that.

JOANNE *(finding that funny):* How can you possibly be so enamored with a new school building? I think someone desperately needs a beau. *(This throws* JOANNE *and* MARY *into giggles behind their hands.)*

ALICE: Oh, you two have as much imagination as a stone.

MARY: Maybe she needs a "Neanderthal" to drag her away by the hair. *(Again, the girls fly into giggles.)*

JOANNE: She's probably waiting for Henry to beat his chest in her direction. (JOANNE *giggles again, but* MARY *stops and frowns.)*

MARY: That's not very funny.

JOANNE *(trying to subdue her giggles):* Sorry.

ALICE: I'm going to pray.

MARY/JOANNE: What?

ALICE: I'm going to pray for this school and its future. Our future.

JOANNE *(still trying to control herself):* Oh, Alice! You're so silly. This isn't a church, it's a school.

(ALICE *moves center stage, arranges her dress appropriately, and goes to her knees clasping her hands in front of her.)*

ALICE: You may join me or not, but I think that the future is ours to shape and this is how I choose to begin.

MARY: I don't believe you. *(She giggles and walks to the door to see if anyone is coming.)*

ALICE *(praying):* Dear God. I've always thought that You placed us on earth to love You and to care for each other. I think that one way I can do both right now is to pray for this wonderful new school You've given us. *(JOANNE makes a stifled grunt sound, trying to stop herself from giggling again.)* I pray, Lord, that You'll help us see the potential for futures here. You'll help us, in this very room, to forge the faith and ideals that will carry us and each proceeding class forward. Thank You for our teachers, our families, and for Your love. Amen. *(ALICE looks up, and both of her friends are looking at her with stifled grins.)*

MARY: Hallelujah. *(Both girls giggle)*

ALICE *(standing):* All right. I'll go now and leave you two to your musing about the uppercavemen . . . oops . . . I mean upperclassmen. *(She exits with a smile.)*

(MARY and JOANNE remain in the classroom and move stage right. As they begin to speak, two more girls, SUE and LYNN, appear at the door. The two at the door are dressed in '50s knee-length dresses, and it is apparent that as they look around to see if the classroom is empty, they do not see MARY and JOANNE.)

JOANNE: So, now that Miss High and Mighty is gone, you must tell me about your date with Henry.

SUE *(looking about room):* The coast is clear.

MARY: It was delightful.

LYNN *(pushing SUE in):* Well, get in there before someone sees us in the hall.

MARY: We went with the Swenson twins and their dates. I really wish you and Martin could have come.

LYNN: All right. So what's the story about Friday night?

(As LYNN and SUE move stage center, two more girls, RAZZ and CHEZ, appear at the door looking around and they as well see the room as empty. They enter. These girls are dressed in typical '80s grunge with multi-colored shock hairstyles.)

RAZZ: So move your shanks in the door before somebody sees it ain't locked. What ya want . . . an invitation?

SUE: Well . . .

CHEZ: Shut up!

(From here until the end of the scene each pair of girls are aware only of each oth-

er. They ask their questions and give their answers, and each pair pause, until all of their counterparts "in time" respond appropriately in their given sections of the stage, but never move to distract attention from any character speaking.)

JOANNE: This is so exciting. I've been beside myself with anticipation.

LYNN: I'm on pins and needles. I can't wait.

RAZZ: All right, cut the happy dribble and spill it.

MARY: That's why I love you so. You're so impatient.

SUE: You're my best friend. I just had to tell you before the day got started.

CHEZ: Shut up!

(JOANNE *giggles at* MARY. LYNN *touches her friend's arm, urging her on.* RAZZ *just rolls her eyes as if to say, "yeah fine, get on with it."*)

MARY: Well, we all had a perfectly lovely time at the theatre. Henry even whispered to me of what a wonderful evening he had. I'm thinking of perhaps letting him hold my hand on our next date. (JOANNE *giggles.*)

SUE: He was so handsome in his pompadour and new leather coat. I nearly fainted away. We saw *Creature from the Black Lagoon* at the drive-in. He even did the old Armstrong heater thing. He was so cute. (LYNN *sighs.*)

CHEZ: OK. No big deal, right! I'm not going to bear his child or nothing. We made out at my place for an hour, then my parents kicked us out . . . so we went to the club to bash heads for a while. All sorta boring. (RAZZ *belches.*)

JOANNE *(giggles):* I think he's so handsome and strong. You make a beautiful couple.

MARY: I think he looks like my father. To be honest, that's my criteria. It's quite a lofty goal, but I'm looking for a beau just like father. (JOANNE *sighs.*)

LYNN: I think he looks like Elvis. Ohhh . . . those eyes.

SUE: Maybe. Of course my father thinks all my dates look like Elvis. He calls them "street trash." He probably wants me to marry someone like him. (LYNN *makes a face.*)

RAZZ: He's got sort of a gut, but I think he looks like that old rocker . . . Mick Jagger.

CHEZ: Gross. That's my father. He had a fling with my mother back in the stone ages. You really know how to gag me, don't you!

JOANNE: You're so lucky.

MARY: Who knows what the future may hold. Wedding bells perhaps . . . after college, and only if he's able to provide a decent living. But I'll tell you. I'm keeping my eye on Alice. She doesn't fool me for a minute. I've seen her look at Henry Clermont.

SUE: I'm not sure what to expect. He's certainly cute. *(Half joking)* You just keep your little paws off him.

CHEZ: Whatever. He's yours, if you want 'im.

(The first bell rings and the girls all react to it. JOANNE, MARY, LYNN, and SUE all scamper off to class passing by RAZZ and CHEZ, who clog/slump their way to the door. Before they exit, HAROLD enters dressed in '60s attire of straight-leg jeans and a letter jacket. RAZZ and CHEZ walk out as he sits and starts work on a math paper before him. After a moment BETH, a pretty girl, also in '60s attire, enters.)

BETH *(apparently upset, she sees HAROLD)*: Oh.

HAROLD *(looks up)*: Hi.

BETH *(wiping eyes)*: I'm sorry . . . I'll leave you alone.

HAROLD: Nah. I'm just redoing this math homework. Mrs. Clermont said I need to get this stuff by either practice or osmosis. Whatever that means.

BETH *(waiting to leave)*: Well . . . I . . .

HAROLD: Personally . . . I think it's hopeless. But it's been a quiet lunch. *(Holds up his lunch bag)* Maybe too quiet. Uh . . . wanna banana? Beth, right?

BETH: Yes. I mean, no. (HAROLD *looks at her like "huh."*) I mean, yes, I'm Beth. But no, I don't want anything. Thank you. *(Starts to edge toward the door)*

HAROLD: OK. Hey, wait. Do you know anything about this algebra stuff? I'm in a pickle here.

BETH: Uhm . . . *(Decides to help for just a minute)* Well, I'm pretty good with math. Science is my favorite . . . but . . . *(Crosses to HAROLD)*

HAROLD: Well, math is my worst. I'm never gonna use any of this stuff anyway. Axioms, Xs and Ys . . . what happened to plain old numbers?

BETH *(looking at his paper)*: Algebra really isn't all that hard. You just have to think of the letters like numbers. *(Points to paper)* See, with this one, all you have to do is multiply this number by this one and Y by this one. The rest is simple.

HAROLD: These two?

BETH *(leaning close over HAROLD's shoulder)*: Uh-huh . . . you see the Y goes over this one. So then you'd divide these two here.

HAROLD *(makes a little sense now)*: Oh. Yeah . . . OK. Thanks. *(Smiles up at BETH and for the first time they realize just how close they are to each other.)*

BETH (*taking a step back, a little embarrassed*): So . . . uh . . . it's really not that hard. You'll get it.

HAROLD: Yeah, yeah . . . Thanks.

BETH: Well . . . I'd better leave you alone so you can finish this. (*Not going*) Bye. (*Starts to go*)

HAROLD: No. Please. This is great (*indicating math paper*), but I think I've reached my math limit for the day anyway. (*Looks at wall clock*) Look, there's 15 minutes of lunch period left. So I can scramble out if you need to do something in here.

BETH: You don't have to. I was just trying to get away by myself for a while. That's all.

HAROLD: Guess I messed that up, huh? (*Gathering his stuff*) I'll scoot.

BETH (*making up her mind about something*): Let's . . . (HAROLD *looks at her*) . . . we might as well both stay here till lunch is over. I guess I'm a little hungry . . . if your offer is still open.

HAROLD: Sure. We'll make it a private banquet and gab about math axioms.

(*They sit and divide up* HAROLD's *remaining lunch and look at each other for a moment. Clearly there's a spark of attraction here, but neither is sure what to do with it.*)

HAROLD: I'm Harold, by the way.

BETH: I know. We've got science together.

HAROLD: Right. But, I thought . . . well, since we never really . . . met before . . . I just (*Beat*) . . . you are really good at science. A real Braniac.

BETH: Thanks.

HAROLD (*back stepping*): I didn't mean that in a mean way. I guess, you're just really smart. I think that's neat.

BETH (*smiling*): It's OK. Thanks.

(*After another long silence* HAROLD *takes a stab at conversation.*)

HAROLD: Uh . . . I saw you and Jack Dugan at the pep rally last Friday.

BETH (*suddenly subdued*): Really?

HAROLD: Yeah. He's a pretty neat guy. (*Pause, as he figures out how to say this*) Uhmm . . . you two been dating long?

BETH: Too long! He's a jerk.

HAROLD (*pause, feeling sort of stupid*): Uh . . . well, I wasn't saying he was a great guy. (BETH *gives him a look that says, "Shut up, now."*) Or anything bad either. I had just seen you two . . . but it's really none of my business. *(Awkward silence)* So science is your favorite, huh?

BETH *(upset, not looking at* HAROLD*)*: Jack and I broke up. It happened today at lunch, so I'd rather not talk about it. All right?

HAROLD: Sure.

(Another long pause, then HAROLD *tries again.)*

HAROLD: Hey, what did you think of that air-raid drill this morning? Was that something, or what? I was right in the middle of math class, so the timing couldn't have been more perfect.

BETH *(very serious):* Oh, I hate those.

HAROLD *(feeling even more stupid):* Well . . . yeah, me too . . . I just thought . . .

BETH *(interrupting):* It just makes my heart stop whenever those sirens go off. All I can think of is how this might be the last breath I ever breathe. It terrifies me.

HAROLD *(feeling really stupid now):* Oh boy.

BETH *(uncomfortable):* Maybe we should go. It's almost time for class. *(Starts getting up)*

HAROLD: I'm sorry, Beth. I keep saying all kinds of dumb stuff. I'm usually not such a jerk. It's just . . . I don't know. I'm so dumb.

BETH *(stops):* You're not being dumb. It's my fault. I'm tied up in knots about . . . what happened at lunch. I thought I loved him. Then in one fell swoop he just . . . *(Pause)* I'm sorry. You don't want to hear this.

HAROLD: No, really . . . it's OK. If you want to talk about it. I mean, people seem to do that with me. I even sorta like it. I've got a preacher's face or something, I guess. *(Beat)* If Jack dumped you, he was the jerk, in my opinion . . . that is.

BETH: Thank you. *(Beat)* You do have a nice face. (HAROLD *smiles, looks away, slightly embarrassed.)* Harold. *(He looks at her.)* What do you think about?

HAROLD: Huh?

BETH: When the air-raid drills happen. What do you think about?

HAROLD: Oh . . . I don't know. What about you?

BETH: For me . . . *(She stops herself.)* . . . Oh never mind. You probably wouldn't understand.

HAROLD: Hey, it's OK. I'm in the drama club. I'll act like I understand. *(She looks puzzled.)* It's a joke. Sorry. Really, what do you think about?

BETH: I think about what Mr. Carter told us in science class. About Hiroshima, and the A-bomb, the equivalent of 200,000 tons of dynamite. A four-square mile radius obliterated, over 100,000 casualties.

HAROLD: Yeah . . . I remember.

BETH: Every time I hear that siren, I think of thousands and thousands of people . . . with no faces.

HAROLD: No faces?

BETH: I've even had nightmares about it. As if the bomb left them all there but blew their faces off. And I'm one of them. In my dream, I see me trying to scream, but I . . . I can't because there's nothing there. I'm faceless; I'm nothing. And it's all controlled by some person with his finger on a button.

(Long silence as this sets in)

HAROLD *(pause):* I guess . . . I think about God. (BETH *gives him a questioning look.)* I mean, for me, it comes down to what's really important.

BETH: What do you mean?

HAROLD: Well . . . when I think about this life being . . . over, I've got to go back to what's really important. The people I love, you know, my family, and . . . God. My dad says God is really the one in control, and I think that's true.

BETH: You really believe that?

HAROLD *(pause):* Yeah. I guess the only stuff that's really worthwhile is . . . who you love and maybe in doing good stuff for people. You know, stuff God would want.

BETH: I never thought about it that way.

HAROLD: When you think about God being in control and there being a heaven and stuff, then it's sorta easier to not be afraid, I guess.

(After a brief pause, BETH *leans over and kisses* HAROLD *on the cheek.)*

HAROLD *(surprised):* What was . . . ?

BETH: I like your thoughts a lot better than mine. Can I borrow yours?

HAROLD: Sure. *(Touches cheek)* They're yours . . . paid in full.

BETH *(starting to get up):* No, I still owe you. How about a few tutoring sessions in algebra.

HAROLD: Good enough. But I'm afraid it'll be like trying to resuscitate a dead man. (BETH *makes a face.)* Oops. Sorry, bad pun under the circumstances, I guess.

*(*BETH *smiles at him as they begin gathering their things to exit. Two boys enter wearing '70s clothes. One,* TED, *has very long dirty hair, a tie-dyed T-shirt and an*

Army shirt, with patch covered, very beat-up bell-bottom jeans. The other one, ROY, *has a zipper front shirt and stripped bells, all very neat and clean.)*

TED: So what you in for, man? Erasing the blackboard too fast?

ROY: Me?

TED: No him. *(Pointing to no one)*

ROY: Well . . . I was . . . talking in class.

TED: Whoa! Now there's a major felony, man. I'm surprised they didn't like, slap your wrist while they were at it.

ROY *(trying to fit in):* Ha. Yeah.

TED *(smiles and shakes his head):* Me, I'm a terminal case. Deadhead too. *(Holds out his hand)*

ROY *(looks at his hand, then understands and he tentatively slaps* TED's *palm):* I'm Roy.

TED: Yeah, I know who you are. Boy wonder, uncle wise kid. Don't see many "Goody Two-shoes" in detention, though. That's what you are, right? You're like . . . teacher's pet. Huh, man?

ROY *(defensively):* No. Not really.

TED: Hey. No sweat. I'm not climbing your tree. Just saying it like it is.

ROY *(uncomfortable pause):* Uh . . . I'm supposed to be doing homework, so . . .

TED: Oh, yeah, better do what you're told. Don't want "the man" busting your chops. Cool. Look, I'm just gonna light up, so, don't mind me. *(Starts rummaging around in his pockets)*

ROY: In here?

TED: Hey, it's cool. Just got a little leftover roach here. I'll open the window, though. Wouldn't want to stain your virgin lungs. *(Moves over toward the window)*

ROY *(looking at the door):* Look, Mrs. Clermont will probably be back any minute.

TED: It's cool, Goody. If worse comes to worse, I'll just eat the evidence. Who knows, maybe the fickle finger of fate will strike, and she'll think the smell is coming from you, man. That'd be cool.

ROY: No. I don't think so.

TED *(suddenly becoming a little aggressive, he walks toward* ROY): What? You gonna play the heavy with me, Goody? You tellin' me no? You wanta tell me something?

ROY: I was saying . . .

TED: I know all about you . . . sweet, little choirboy. (ROY *looks surprised.*) Oh, yeah, I spy, man. You go to my old lady's church. She dragged me there one week. There you were, pretty as a peach.

ROY: I don't want any trouble, Ted.

TED: Who's talking trouble? I'm talking GOD, man. God is DEAD. Don't you read the papers, Goody? There it was bold as brass. God is Dead. Deceased. Kaput!

ROY: This isn't . . .

TED: Hey, I'm just sayin' it as it is, man. *(Turns a chair around and sits on it backward facing* ROY*)* But now I'm thinkin, since you won't let me mellow out, you need to tell me, why do you go sit with all that boring garbage, man, when God is dead?

ROY: Well . . . they're just wrong, I guess.

TED: So why go, man? A chick. Is it a chick?

ROY: No. I mean the papers are wrong.

TED: The *Times?* How can the *Times* be wrong, man?

ROY: It just is, I think. God can't die. I mean, Jesus did, but that's because He chose to.

TED *(snorts):* Now that's too heavy for me, man. It's all just freaky. Are you freaky, Goody?

ROY: No.

TED *(looks at him a second):* OK, here's this. My brother, right? He bit it in Vietnam. He goes over there for God and his country. We're in the right, right? We're the good guys. So, if God ain't dead, how does it all fit? Huh? *(Almost angry)* It blows my mind, man. You guys can sit there and tell me . . . what? Why did God let my brother fry. He was good. He was good.

ROY: I . . . I don't know.

TED *(quiet now, beat):* See, there it is, Goody. Nobody knows. Nobody. But I know what you can do with it. *(He turns the chair back around and sits down facing away from* ROY.*)*

ROY: It's not God's fault. (TED *looks back at him.*) I don't think you can blame God for all the crazy, stupid stuff we do here on earth. That's the point, really. He's not standing up there with a big hammer to smash us when we screw up. We screw up and end up smashing ourselves. And He says, "OK, if that's what you want." See, I think He wants us to do better in life and even offers to help but lets us make the choices. *(Beat)* And, if your brother was good, like you say, then maybe he knew about God's desires, and maybe he made the right choices and that's why he was good. And even though something wrong happened to him, his right choice means he's OK now too.

TED *(pause):* You know, Goody . . . that's just freaky enough that it almost makes sense. *(*TED *smiles.)* You're OK, Goody. I still think you're freaky, but you're cool. Hey, you want a toke on this roach? *(Starts digging in his shirt again)*

ROY: Uh . . . no. I don't think so.

TED *(decides not to find it):* Yeah, OK, it'll hold. *(Turns back around and puts his feet up on the desk)*

(Two boys, NICK *and* PETE, *dressed in average '90s apparel with backpacks enter looking around to see that the coast is clear. The passing bell rings.* TED *and* ROY *get up.* TED *holds his hand out.* ROY *slaps him five.* ROY *gathers his stuff, and he and* TED *exit.)*

(In hushed tones)

NICK: Sup?

PETE: I got it.

NICK: You got it? No! How did you . . . *(Checks out the door)* Where is it?

PETE: Here. *(Pats jacket)*

NICK: You got it with you? *(Incredulous, loud)* No way! *(They both look at the open door, then move to the teacher's desk on the other side of the classroom.)* No way. They catch you and you're history, man. No ifs, ands, or buts. *(*JOE *saunters in on the last part of* NICK's *dialogue and catches on that something's up.)*

JOE: Hey.

NICK: He got it.

JOE *(taken aback):* As if.

PETE: Here. *(Pats jacket)*

JOE *(checks the door):* You're whacked. Show me, Pete.

NICK: No, don't.

PETE: Sure. *(Opens jacket a little so that* JOE *can look in.* NICK *runs back to check the hallway, nervously, but can't help to steal a quick glance in* PETE's *coat.)*

NICK: Oh man. He's really got it. Ya gotta hide it, man.

JOE *(to* PETE): You're money! You are money, guy!

(LINK *sticks his head in the door.*)

LINK: What's up, yo?

NICK *(back to* PETE*)*: Come on. Not him.

PETE: Sure, why not?

LINK: What?

NICK *(nervous):* He got it.

LINK *(catching that something's exciting but not really sure what):* Cool! What?

JOE: In his coat. *(To* PETE*)* You are money!

LINK: Le'me see! Le'me see! *(Moving to* PETE*)*

NICK *(still at door):* Hey, hey! Cool it!

(They all strike a nonchalant pose as a STUDENT *enters the room. He walks to the teacher's desk, looking at the guys, puts a paper down and then exits. A pause.)*

LINK: What?

*(*PETE *opens his jacket slightly, the boys gather around and coolly all take a quick glance. They all break into male crowing and celebratory shoves, punches, and struts, slapping* PETE *on the back with general enthusiasm. Suddenly, they all strike a nonchalant pose again and lean up against the desk as a couple more students enter the room. After seeing the guys, though, they decide to exit again and wait for the bell.)*

LINK *(to the guys):* What?

JOE: Didn't you see?

LINK: He's got on a shirt. *(*JOE *smacks him.)* It's a nice shirt.

JOE: Nah. *(Whispers to him)*

LINK: Here? In school? *(With respect)* Oh . . . dude.

JOE: He's the king. *(Can't believe it)* Cool.

NICK: How, man! How'd you get it?

PETE: Easy. My father keeps it in the cabinet in his study. I just walked in and . . . POP . . . it was mine. In my bag it went. On the bus, I stuffed it in the back of my pants. *(The boys listen in rapt silence as if this is the beginning of lore.)* And, then, I walked right by old McGrunt, himself. He even checks my bag, right? I just smiled, real cool, then I walked in here. Easy.

(The next three lines are spoken together.)

JOE: You are the king. The king.

NICK: Man. No way.

LINK: Fly. Totally fly.

NICK: Aren't you afraid they'll skank you?

PETE: Nicky boy, afraid isn't in my vocabulary. Now. *(Pats his jacket)*

(The next three lines are spoken together.)

JOE: The king!

NICK: Aw, man!

LINK: Dude. You got that!

LINK: What about your old man? Won't he miss his property?

PETE: He hardly ever looks at it. By the time he thinks about it again, I'll have it back in place. I've got it all figured.

JOE *(excited)*: Wait'll they find out you've got it, man. You'll be . . .

PETE: Whoa. Find out? Nobody's gonna find out.

JOE: Yeah . . . but I mean . . .

PETE *(makes a disqualifying buzzer sound)*: This is for us. Nobody else.

LINK: So what's the scheme, dude?

PETE: Use it. Nobody has to even see it to know we've got it. *(Points to his temple)* It's here, right? We'll know we've got the power and we'll use it. We'll hit 'em with it. We have to.

NICK *(nervously)*: We'll?

PETE: You know it. It's for you guys too. They've got all their junk. Well now we've got this. But this is power. Our power.

(All the boys start their crowing and punching again. Immediately they stop and strike their cool poses as JULIE walks in the classroom door.)

JULIE: All right, you posers. What's going on?

PETE: Uh . . . hi, Julie. What's up?

JULIE: Everybody knows you guys are sneakin' in here, droolin' over something. Probably, something really stupid. So before some brain dead teacher drifts in here and strings you up, you'd better tell me what it is so I can save your sorry, scabby-looking hides.

(The whole group just stares at her. Long pause.)

LINK: What?

JULIE: Oh, that's smooth. The fact that you make him your spokesperson says a lot, Pete. OK. What'd you do? Sneak a *National Geographic* in here, or is it a Victoria's Secret catalog?

JOE *(disgruntled with her teasing):* Yeah . . . well. It's a lot bigger than that. *(Referring to* PETE*)* He's the king.

JULIE: Oh. You doing an Elvis thing now, Petey? Are these your Pips?

PETE: Look, Julie. *(Obviously taken aback by her presence)* It's just . . . well, you don't really need to . . . I mean I don't think . . .

JULIE: Ha. You're such a jerk. Why did I even bother? *(She turns to leave.)*

PETE: No! I've got something that's gonna make a lot of difference around here.

(The next three lines are spoken together.)

JOE: The king.

NICK: Oh, man.

LINK: You got that.

JULIE *(back to* PETE*):* OK, don't tell me. You actually did your homework and you're planning on sending all the teachers into shock.

JOE: It'll shock 'em, all right. They'll sit up and notice when we hit 'em with it. Won't they, Pete?

NICK: Shut up, man!

JULIE *(looks suspiciously at them, trying to figure this out):* Look, the bell is gonna ring any minute now, and Clermont is gonna roll her bulk in here, so stop yankin' my chain. What've you got? *(Really wondering now)* Some sorta weapon?

(The next three lines are spoken together.)

JOE: The king.

LINK: You got that.

NICK *(nervous):* Aw, man.

JULIE: You guys are scary. What? What? Your mom's pepper spray? A pocketknife? Your secret Batarang?

*(*PETE *shakes his head "no," pleased that he actually has* JULIE's *serious attention.)*

PETE: This is serious, Julie. Maybe you'd better drop it.

(The next three lines are spoken together.)

JOE: The king, man.

NICK: Oh, man.

LINK: You got that.

JULIE: Come on. What is it? Just tell me the truth. *(Decides on another tact—she moves seductively to* PETE*)* Hey, there now Petey. *(Walks her fingers up* PETE's *shoulder.)* You can tell little Julie all about it, right? I mean . . . we're close, aren't we?

PETE *(completely flustered):* Uh . . .

NICK: No, no, no!

LINK: Don't do it, dude.

*(*PETE *smiles and slowly opens his jacket.* JULIE *winks, looks in, and then grabs at the jackets contents.)*

JULIE: Gimme that.

(The boys all stare in shock as JULIE *pulls a Bible out of* PETE's *jacket.)*

JULIE: A Bible! *(She starts dancing toward the door.)* They've got a Bible! A BI-BLE!

(The boys rush to get her to be quiet and give back the Bible.)

(The next four lines are spoken together.)

NICK: No, No! Cut it out!

PETE: Be quiet!

JOE: Give it! Give it!

LINK: Oh, dude.

(They wrestle her to the ground, regain the Bible, and move back.)

JULIE: Ha, ha. You stoners are rich.

*(*MRS. CLERMONT *enters and moves to her desk. No one seems to notice her.)*

JULIE: A gun I could see. They might suspend you for a week. But a Bible . . . they'll string you up till you turn 30. You're dead meat. *(She gets up, they just look at her—suddenly she rushes for the door.)* Hey, everybody, guess what? *(She exits and the boys all follow her out yelling and pleading.)*

*(*MRS. CLERMONT *sits at her desk and stares out the window. Two '90s students,* ANITA *and* MICK, *enter.)*

ANITA: Sorry we're late, Mrs. Clermont.

CLERMONT: Oh, no problem today, of all days. How are you two?

ANITA: OK.

MICK: Nothing much doin', but hangin' today, Mrs. C. Sup with you?

CLERMONT: I haven't been extremely busy myself . . . just revisiting a lot of memories, I suppose.

MICK: Yeah. Been a long year, that's for true. I thought we'd never be done with it.

CLERMONT: Well, I'm not speaking of just this year. I mean all the years I've spent in this school building. Memories flit by . . . some as a student and then as a teacher. I've been around for quite awhile. As I'm sure you'd put it, "I'm old as dirt."

MICK: Hey, I never said that, Mrs. C. Somebody tell you I said that? (MRS. CLERMONT *smiles and shakes her head "no."*)

ANITA *(she slaps MICK on the arm):* So here we are. Last day. What'll we do?

MICK: Yeah, is it the rack again or just whips and fractions?

CLERMONT: Neither one today. This is it. You've both worked very hard and pulled your grades up to Cs. Marginal for you, I'm afraid, Mr. Ludens, but we'll nudge it into place for good behavior.

MICK: Great. So that's it, huh? Great. My dad always said there were such things as miracles.

ANITA: Thanks, Mrs. Clermont.

CLERMONT: I didn't cancel our meeting though because I wanted you both to know that I appreciated all the hard work you've put in to pass this course. I know it was difficult at times, but I promise you that education always pays off. *(Pause as the two kids just look at her)* I also wanted to say good-bye, I suppose. I don't often get to say good-byes to my students. The last day always seems to leave things somewhat unraveled.

MICK: Hey, I heard you were gonna vamoose after this year. Gold watch time, huh? (ANITA *smacks him on the arm.)* What?

CLERMONT *(a little saddened):* Yes. This was my last year. Out with the old, in with the new . . . as the saying goes.

MICK *(unaware of MRS. CLERMONT's demeanor):* Speaking of new . . . how 'bout that new building, huh? I scoped it out. Old Smitty says they'll have heated floors in the locker rooms, massage tables, and a whirlpool. That's gonna make my senior year.

ANITA *(throws a look at MICK):* Sorry to see you go, Mrs. Clermont.

CLERMONT: Well, thank . . .

MICK: I mean, it puts this dump to shame. I'm just glad they're gonna board this hole up before I graduate.

CLERMONT: Sometimes it's easier to dismiss something that's . . . that needs some work, but there's so much about this school that will be missed, I'm sure.

MICK: Yeah. I'll miss being baked like a potato in the summer and deep frozen in the winter, that's for sure. I even heard the new school's got indoor plumbing. *(Chuckles at his wit)*

CLERMONT: What about its history?

MICK: Huh?

CLERMONT: Think of what this school has seen, Mr. Luden. Can you envision the thousands of students that have walked these school halls and grown in its embrace? Young people, like you, who have made their way in this sometimes harsh world, because of what was, with hope and love, offered and accepted in these very rooms. Day after day, year after year . . . lives enriched, minds challenged, dreams forged.

MICK *(long pause, as* MICK *looks at* MRS. CLERMONT): Yeah . . . sure. Are we gonna get our grades in the mail, or can I pick 'em up here?

CLERMONT *(puzzled):* Grades?

MICK: Yeah, I gotta prove to my old man that I passed so he'll let me get car insurance this summer?

CLERMONT: In the mail.

MICK *(gets up to leave):* Yeah, well, I guess that's in a couple'a weeks. So that's great. Can we go?

CLERMONT: Certainly.

MICK: Great! You comin', Nita?

(ANITA nods and MICK exits.)

(MRS. CLERMONT turns and looks back out the window. ANITA gets up. She's very much aware of MRS. CLERMONT, but she is unsure if there's something she should say. She stops at the door.)

ANITA: Mrs. Clermont?

CLERMONT *(looks quietly back to ANITA):* Yes, Mrs. Rodrigues?

ANITA: You can call me, Anita. I know you're sort of formal about those things, but I guess it's OK on the last day, right?

CLERMONT: I'm a little old-fashioned, I suppose. Anita, you can call me . . . Alice.

ANITA: OK . . . Alice. *(Pause)* Anyway, I wanted to say . . . thanks. When we were alone, I mean . . . *(Looks toward the door and back)* See, I know I'm not the smartest or anything, but in here it was always . . . different, I guess.

CLERMONT: You mean, math class?

ANITA: No. Math's a real . . . it's very hard. No, it's . . . you. You made it easier. Math and just school, too, I guess. Maybe I'm not making sense.

CLERMONT: I think I understand. *(She smiles.)* Thank you, Anita.

ANITA *(she smiles back)*: Sure. *(She starts to walk out, then turns back.)* God bless you, Mrs. Clermont.

CLERMONT *(surprised)*: You can't say that in school, I'm afraid, Anita.

ANITA: Sure I can. Especially here. Bye.

CLERMONT: Good-bye.

(ANITA exits. MRS. CLERMONT sits at her desk for a moment. She walks to the window and looks out. She turns back, thoughtfully, to face the room and smiles. Fade to black.)

JUST CALL ME MARK

by
Jim Custer

Setting:

The action takes place in many areas. This piece was originally conceived to be done with minimal props and areas isolated by spotlights. When the character of Mark is addressing the audience in one of his monologues, it should be done center stage. The character of the Mother and the Counselor should be in the same area each time, also. All the other scenes should alternate between stage right and stage left. Use your whole stage. This piece should be very fast-paced.

Characters:

MARK: *Mark is 16 and a bit of a loner. He dresses in black and has a quick wit. He is searching and most of all "wants to belong."*

JENNIFER: *Jennifer is 16 and comes from a strong home. She is very together and takes a quick liking to Mark. She goes to a different high school than either Mark or Sean.*

SEAN: *Sean is 17, has his own car, is a little preppie in his dress and attitude. He and Jennifer go to the same church. He likes Jennifer; he just hasn't told her.*

MOTHER: *She is Mark's mother. She is divorced and has a habit of rattling on about nothing. She is worldly in her outlook but loves her son very much.*

COUNSELOR: *He is a professional with a dry tone. About 50 years old.*

RONNIE: *An obnoxious friend of Sean's. They've known each other since they were kids. He is loud, opinionated, and a bully.*

PEG: *A friend, if not something more to Ronnie. She is somewhat "tomboyish" in her approach.*

DAVID: *He is Ronnie's friend and follows his lead.*

FATHER: *He is Mark's father and left his son with a damaging memory.*

PASTOR: *Even though he is in Mark's imagination, he is very real. He is broad in his character. A definite hell-and-brimstone person.*

EXTRAS: *Assorted youth to fill in the gaps. They play church people, carnival barkers, teachers, and youth in the youth group.*

Props:

Make it as simple as you can. For the furniture, car, pews, and bleachers, use folding chairs. For the table in the counselor's office, use a box. You will need a jar full of pencils, a Bible, two phones, an educator's pointer, carnival music, gospel organ music, very traditional organ music, a horn honk, offstage sounds for the church scene, and a whistle.

The scene in the youth room should be done by miming activities that go on (i.e., Ping-Pong tables, air hockey, watching a TV, etc.).

47

(At rise, the show starts out in the black. The voice of a teenage boy is heard.)

MARK: Being a teenager stinks. Ultimately, it is some great cosmic someone's idea of a joke. Knock, knock. Who's there? Teenager. Teenager, who? Teenager you. *(Buzzer sound)* And you lose!

(We hear carnival music and a spotlight comes up. A teenage guy is sitting on a stool facing the audience. A crowd of people are standing around looking and listening to the barker, as you would at a carnival arcade.)

BARKER: Ladies and gentlemen! Step right up and have the time of your life. For only 25 cents, you can play connect the dots with this young man's face. That's right! Do it correctly, there's a secret message and a fabulous prize. *(The group excitedly moves forward waving money. We go to a blackout and hear the voice over again.)*

MARK: Last week, I had a zit that I swear looked like a two-ton tomato. I pretended it wasn't there, but when it's large enough your mom starts calling it for dinner . . . you have to pay attention.

(Lights come up and we have a teenage guy and girl standing completely motionless, as if they are mannequins, in front of a class. A teacher, in a lab coat, is holding a pointer and is talking.)

TEACHER: Class. What we have here is Adolescents Conspicuous . . . male and female. Notice the wide, empty space between the ears, the glaze over the eyes, gangly stems, with oversized appendages. Also notice the outer wear designed to make a statement and annoy parents.

CLASS: Oooo.

TEACHER *(looks at them with a grave expression):* There is no cure.

CLASS *(gasp)*

(Blackout)

MARK: I wanted to make a statement, so I grew a goatee . . . only you couldn't see it. So I darkened it with my sister's mascara. It rained, and it all ran down my neck. *(Beat)* Turn on the light. *(Spotlight hits him.)* Thanks. Hi, I'm Mark. Actually, my real name is Marion, Marion Kay Riddle. Yep, Marion, as in Maid Marion, Kay as in K-A-Y, my parents wanted a girl, and Riddle, as in a joke or confusing puzzle with a surprising end. And that's pretty much how I see myself. I'm not sure about the surprising end, but the confusing puzzle and joke seem to be accurate. Hence my wearing of black. I am a walking "black comedy." I shortened my name to Mark in the fourth grade after I'd heard "Marion the Farion" for the 30 millionth time. It seemed more direct, succinct *(beat),* and it kept me out of fights. But, life has gotten a lot more complicated since then. I tried to talk to my mom about it.

(Light comes up on a woman who is Mark's MOTHER.)

MOTHER *(she speaks very fast and moves from one phrase to another without really thinking):* I know, honey. There's all these feelings, mixed with all that other stuff . . . grades, school, drugs, sex. My father called it the Hormonal Highway leading straight to hell . . . girls, etc., etc., etc. Just a confusing time . . . confusing, confusing, confusing. *(Beat)* How about tofu for dinner?

(Lights go out on MOTHER, *and* MARK *looks back to the audience.)*

MARK: She tries. *(Beat)* Oh, my parents? They're divorced. *(Pause, thinking)* I think they're divorced . . . anyway, he's gone. "He," being my father. I remember the last thing he said to me.

(Spot comes up on a man who is obviously Mark's FATHER.)

FATHER: You're about as worthless as a 4-foot sack of horse manure.

(Blackout on the FATHER)

MARK: Whatever. *(Beat)* One day he just disappeared. He left Mom with three kids *(pointing to himself)* . . . the oldest, a dog, a mortgage, $25.00 in the bank, and me with the name Marion. *(Imitating Mr. Rogers)* Do you know how to spell dysfunctional?

(Lights come up on a COUNSELOR, *in a chair, with Mark's* MOTHER *across from him. There is a jar of pencils on the coffee table in front of the couch.* MARK *walks into the scene and sits next to his mom.)*

COUNSELOR: You are a complicated young man, Marion. But what I sense is some inner anger. What do you think?

MARK *(raises his hand and it's as if time has stopped; everyone freezes except* MARK, *who then addresses the audience):* I do this for my mom.

*(*MARK *drops his hand and time starts up again. This theatrical device will be used throughout the rest of the piece.)*

COUNSELOR: Marion?

MARK *(he picks up a pencil and breaks it):* What?

COUNSELOR: Is there any inner anger?

MOTHER *(speaking slow and concerned at first, then getting more heated and passionate as she talks):* Yes dear . . . is there? Anger? Deep down inside . . . ready to, sort of bubble up, like a volcano . . . bubbling, bubbling, bubbling . . . like Mount St. Helens?

COUNSELOR: Ms. Riddle?

MOTHER *(ignoring):* Vesuvius, Krakatoa East of Java.

COUNSELOR: Ms. Riddle.

MOTHER *(not responding to the doctor):* It's understandable, sweetheart. It's not something you have to hide. Just let it out! Let it all out about your father leaving. The slimeball!

COUNSELOR: Excuse me, Ms. Riddle.

MOTHER *(really heated):* The betrayal! The devil-may-care attitude that says "I'm important and all the rest of you people are just trash! Trash to be walked away from . . ."

COUNSELOR: Ms. Riddle.

MOTHER: "Far, far, far away . . ."

COUNSELOR: Uh . . .

MOTHER: "Swept under the carpet . . . trampled underfoot!"

COUNSELOR: Ms. Riddle, get a . . .

MOTHER *(very passionate):* I mean, who cares that I put you through college, had all the children, cooked all the dinners! I mean "whatever"! SO WHAT!

COUNSELOR: Ms. Riddle . . . uh, calm . . .

MOTHER *(quickly changing to a calm person, as if nothing had happened):* Sorry. *(Calmly correcting)* Oh, it's Riddle-Tune.

COUNSELOR: Huh?

MOTHER: It's Riddle-Tune. I took back my maiden name. Riddle-Tune *(beat)* with a hyphen.

COUNSELOR *(looking at her, totally confused):* Oh. *(To* MARK*)* Marion . . . look at me, Marion. *(*MARK *looks and breaks another pencil.)* Better. Now, let's sort of play a game.

MOTHER *(breaking in):* Charades? I was always wonderful as a kid at charades.

COUNSELOR *(getting control):* Well, no, actually . . . a word game. Marion, why don't you just say the first word that comes to mind . . .

MARK *(holding up his hand; time stops):* I'm not sure he wants to know the word on my mind. *(Drops his hand)*

COUNSELOR *(in midsentence as if there wasn't a break):* after I . . . say a word? Can we do that?

*(*MARK *breaks a pencil.)*

(This next segment should start slow and build in rhythm until the last lines.)

COUNSELOR: OK. Now, ready, Marion?

MARK *(breaks a pencil):* Mark.

COUNSELOR: Parent.

MARK: Mark.

COUNSELOR: Alone.

MARK: Mark. *(Breaks a pencil)*

COUNSELOR: Revenge.

MARK: Mark.

COUNSELOR: Siblings.

MARK: Mark. *(Breaks a pencil)*

COUNSELOR: Anger.

MARK: Mark.

COUNSELOR: School.

MARK: Mark. *(Breaks a pencil)*

COUNSELOR: Classmates.

MARK: Mark.

COUNSELOR: Hostility.

MARK: Mark. *(Breaks a pencil)*

COUNSELOR *(beat, then he picks up all the broken pencils on the table):* Interesting.

MARK *(beat):* Mark. *(Breaks another pencil and tosses it on the table.* MARK *and the* COUNSELOR *look at each other.)*

(Lights come up on five people . . . RONNIE, SEAN, DAVID, JENNIFER, PEG. *They are at a basketball game.* RONNIE *and* DAVID *are definitely into it.)*

RONNIE: U-G-L-Y, you ain't got no alibi . . . (DAVID *joins him.)* Yo, ugly! Yo, ugly!

RONNIE: Miss it! *(The team makes it.)* Ah! Lucky shot! *(To his team,* DAVID *joins and they ad-lib things they would yell at their own team.)* OK, let's go! Get it in!

SEAN: C'mon!

JENNIFER: Let's go, Wildcats!

SEAN *(looking at* JENNIFER *in approval):* All right. Go, Wildcats.

RONNIE: OK, throw it! He's open . . . half court! He's open. *(General ad-lib)* C'mon . . . watch it! He's behind . . . Watch! *(The other team steals the ball.)*

Ah, man! Stop him! Stop him! *(The other team makes the shot.)* Ah! C'mon, guys, you're playing like women!

PEG *(to* RONNIE*)*: Watch it.

RONNIE: They are! They're playin' like women.

PEG *(to* JENNIFER*)*: Do you ever wonder how the species has continued to exist?

DAVID: OK . . . let's go! Take your time . . . take your . . . OK! NOW GO! He's open! In the corner. All right, go! Go! *(They all yell as their team is about to score.)* Two on three! *(They are really yelling, and their team makes it.)* All right! Did you see that? Stuff? Stuff?

RONNIE *(to the opposing stands)*: Take that! Stuff!

SEAN: Ron . . . calm down, everyone's looking at you.

RONNIE: So. Let 'em look. *(Idea)* Here, I'll give 'em something to look at. *(He turns around and starts to unbuckle his belt as if he's going to "moon" the other stands. Immediately* DAVID, SEAN, JEN, *and* PEG *jump up to stop him.)*

EVERYONE: What are you doing?

SEAN: You want to get us thrown out of here?

RONNIE: It'll teach 'em to look.

PEG: Permanently. They'd all go blind.

(We hear a whistle.)

RONNIE *(catching his attention)*: Foul?! What are you . . . You're blind, ref? How much ya gettin' paid . . . ?

PEG *(interrupting)*: Yo, Bammerwack, shut up! *(Taking charge)* Let's get something to eat. *(Starts to get up)*

DAVID *(getting up)*: Yeah, I'm hungry.

RONNIE *(standing)*: You're always hungry. *(To* DAVID*)* You buyin'?

DAVID: Hey, you owe me.

RONNIE: I owe you nothin'.

DAVID: You owe me $10.00.

(They start to argue.)

PEG *(interrupts them)*: Shut up! I'll buy! Just shut up!

RONNIE: OK. *(To* PEG*)* You buyin', huh? All right. I like this women in charge . . . women buyin' . . . women's lib stuff. *(Loud, to the whole audience)* She's buyin'.

PEG: It's not women's lib . . . it's self-preservation. If you have something in your mouth, then you have to shut up. *(They exit.)*

JENNIFER *(after they leave to* SEAN*)*: Uh . . . maybe if we just climb under the seats . . . no one will notice.

SEAN: Sorry.

JENNIFER: Why do you . . . *(pause)* . . . what I'm trying to . . .

SEAN *(interrupting)*: Why do I hang around with him? Because he's a friend, I guess. Friendship's important to me. Besides, I've gotten used to him.

JENNIFER: Or you're deaf.

SEAN: Huh?

(They laugh.)

SEAN: We grew up together. Our moms worked at the same place, so I saw him every day. He's not always like this.

JENNIFER: Oh.

SEAN: Sometimes he's worse. *(They laugh, then* SEAN *sees* MARK, *who has just entered the scene.)* Mark! Mark! Over here! *(He waves him over.)* What are you doing here?

MARK *(holding up his hand; time stops; he addresses the audience)*: I could say the truth . . . like I needed to get out of the house, or be clever and evasive. *(He drops his hand and time starts up again.)* Just checking out how the preps and jocks live. *(Looking around)* This is it, huh?

SEAN: This is Jennifer. She goes to my church.

MARK *(holding up his hand)*: I might have to get into religion. *(Drops his hand and time starts up again.)* I'm Mark.

SEAN: Oh yeah . . . he's Mark.

JENNIFER: Nice to meet you.

SEAN: Jen goes to West.

MARK: East, West . . . It's school. Right?

JENNIFER *(she smiles)*: Right. Sit.

MARK: I'm just here for a little while.

JENNIFER: It's OK. *(She moves over to give him room.)*

MARK: You sure? It might ruin your reputation.

JENNIFER: I can handle it, and no one knows me here anyway.

53

MARK: Cool. (*He sits next to her.*)

SEAN: Hey, thanks for the help with my calculus.

MARK (*holding up his hand; time stops and he addresses the audience*): OK. I like math. Just one more part of the riddle. (*Drops his hand and time starts up again.*) Sure. Anytime.

SEAN: It really helped.

JENNIFER: You like math?

MARK: Whatever.

JENNIFER: You don't look like a math person.

MARK (*holding up his hand, he addresses the audience*): I wonder what a math person looks like. (*Dropping his hand*) It was either that or take up body piercing. Math seemed the best way to go.

JENNIFER (*looks at him in disbelief, then laughs*): No way!

MARK: OK, I lied. (*He holds up his hand.*) I think she likes me. (*Drops his hand*)

SEAN: We've got mids coming up . . . do you think we could get together next week and just run over a couple of things.

MARK: No problem.

(RONNIE, DAVID, *and* PEG *enter, they are carrying food and drinks.*)

RONNIE (*loud and to the other stands*): We're back . . . miss me?

PEG: Shut up, Ronnie!

RONNIE (*noticing* MARK): Who we got here? No, don't tell me . . . Dracula, Night of the Living Dead . . . uh . . . don't tell me . . .

PEG: Shut . . .

RONNIE (*interrupting*): A loser in black. So, Batman, who invited you?

SEAN: Ronnie, I . . .

MARK: Uh . . . it's OK, I was just going.

RONNIE: Good. Didn't really want to eat with that smell around. Could lose my appetite.

MARK (*under his breath*): I doubt it.

RONNIE: What?

MARK (*raising his hand, he addresses the audience*): OK, I have a choice. I could shut up and say "nothing," or I can repeat what I just said. If I repeat myself, I could be ripped apart and the pieces could be stuffed into my shoes. *(Drops hand and time starts again.)* I doubt it. *(Looking at* RONNIE*)*

RONNIE *(moving toward him):* What are you saying?

SEAN *(jumping up):* Just calm down . . . I invited him. I needed to ask him a question, that's all.

RONNIE: So did you ask it?

SEAN: Yes.

RONNIE: Then he can leave.

*(*SEAN *turns and looks at* MARK. *The message is obvious.)*

MARK: Like I said . . . I was just going.

RONNIE: Bye . . . *(beat, mocking)* Marion.

*(*MARK *turns and looks at him, then at* JENNIFER. *The lights go down on that scene, and a spot comes up center stage.* MARK *walks into the spot.)*

MARK *(beat):* What am I supposed to feel? *(Waiting, as if expecting an answer)* The same old thing is what. OK, wearing black is my choice, trying to appear like things don't bother me . . . is my choice. Changing my name was . . . my choice. But always feeling like I don't fit in . . . ?

JENNIFER *(running into his spot, interrupting):* Mark. Who were you talking to?

MARK: Myself.

JENNIFER: Look. I'm sorry.

MARK: Whatever. *(Looking at her)*

JENNIFER: He's just trash . . .

MARK: Yeah . . . but he's big trash. *(He smiles.)*

JENNIFER *(she smiles):* Why does he treat . . . ?

MARK: Ronnie's always like that. Ever since we were kids. If he didn't understand someone or something . . . he picked a fight with it. My counselor calls it impulsive-aggressive. Says it's trying to control situations to hide insecurities. Personally, I think he's constipated. *(They look at each other and laugh.)*

JENNIFER: Should I tell him that?

MARK: Sure . . . after I dictate my will.

JENNIFER: Well, someone should have said something. I should have said something.

(MARK: *looks at her.*)

JENNIFER: Sean should have.

MARK: Why?

JENNIFER: Because he called you over. *(Trying to come up with reasons)* Because . . . he's your friend.

MARK: He's Ronnie's friend. I just help him with his calculus.

JENNIFER: Well . . . he should . . . I just wished he had . . . I had.

MARK: And I wish I was taller . . .

JENNIFER: Yeah. *(Turning and looking over to where the basketball game was)* I'd better . . .

MARK: Whatever. Hey, give my love to Ronnie.

JENNIFER: Yeah. *(She starts to leave, then she turns and comes back.)* Do you mind if I call you sometime?

MARK: Me?

JENNIFER: For help with my math.

MARK: Sure.

JENNIFER *(starts to leave, then turns back again):* Mark . . . *(Pause)* I . . . uh . . . I think you're . . . interesting.

(JENNIFER *exits and* MARK *turns to the audience.)*

MARK *(smiles):* She thinks I'm interesting. I like that. *(Thinking)* Well, I think I do. *(Thinking)* Interesting. *(Thinking)* Interesting.

(Spot comes on Mark's MOTHER.*)*

MOTHER: Interesting? She said interesting? Ooo, that could mean a lot of things, sweetheart. Oh, yes. You see, for a girl, sometimes it has to do with not knowing all the things to say . . . See, it's all these feelings just swimming around and around and around inside and you're not quite sure what to think or to say . . . to think and say . . . so you just say the first thing that comes out because that is all you can think to say. She could have said handsome. I would have . . . of course, I'm your mother. Or smart, or mysterious . . . or interesting. *(Beat)* How about "meatloaf" . . . *(beat)* without the meat, of course?

(Light goes black and comes up again on MARK*)*

MARK: The more I think about it . . . the more I like it. Interesting.

(Light comes up on JENNIFER, *and she has a phone in her hand.* MARK *picks up one too.)*

JENNIFER: And that's all there is to it?

MARK: That's it . . . *(Listening)* Just think of it that way, and it's simple.

JENNIFER: Thanks. *(Long pause as if neither can think of anything to say)* Mark . . . Sean really feels bad about not saying something the other night.

MARK: Yeah?

JENNIFER: Say, do you want to get together?

MARK: Where?

JENNIFER: Well . . . we could *(trying to ease the suggestion in)* you don't have to, now . . . I won't be offended but if you don't want to, but . . . we could . . . *(Long pause)*

MARK: What, rob old ladies?

JENNIFER *(laughs):* No.

MARK: Let the air out of Ronnie's tires?

JENNIFER: No. Go to my youth group meeting.

MARK: Church?

JENNIFER: Well, it's at my church . . . but it's not, you know . . . church.

(MARK is sort of dumbfounded, quiet.)

JENNIFER: Hello? Hello?

MARK: Yeah . . . I was just . . . church, huh?

JENNIFER *(trying to recover and get herself out of an embarrassing situation):* Well, we can do something else.

MARK *(interrupting):* Sure. I'll go . . . I guess.

JENNIFER: Really?

MARK: I'm not going to have to pray, am I?

JENNIFER: No.

MARK: I don't have a tie or anything . . .

JENNIFER: It's not like that . . . just wear what you wear . . . be you.

MARK: Me, huh? OK. How do I get there.

JENNIFER: It's Wednesday. Sean and I will pick you up. Seven?

MARK: Whatever. *(Lights go out on JENNIFER, MARK is still on the phone.)* Bye. *(Looks out to the audience)* Church. I've never been in one. *(Beat)* What in the world do they do in church?

(Lights come up on a Pastor *preaching. He is very stereotypical and broad. There is gospel organ music in the background. The light is still on* Mark *as he looks into the scene.)*

Pastor: Sin! We have sin! I can smell it! Perversion! Brothers and sisters, there is vile, putrid, hell-deserving sin in the audience *(The group of people in the congregation says things like "Yes!" "Preach it, brother," etc.—it should be very broad.)* I can feel it! I can hear it! I can see it! I can taste it! I can touch it! AND IT IS THERE! *(On that word, he points at* Mark, *who is still in his spot.* Mark *turns and looks behind him. He is thinking the pastor is talking to someone else. Then he turns and points to himself as if saying, "Me?")* You! You with the face of Satan! Sin! Come over here!

*(*Mark *shakes his head no.)*

Pastor *(he bellows):* NOW!

*(*Mark *quickly runs over but is terrified.)*

Pastor *(grabbing him by the hair):* This is the face of sin! What I say to you is REPENT! *(To his congregation)* You say it with me! *(They all say together.)* REPENT!

Mark *(terrified):* Uh . . . OK.

Pastor: What?

Mark: Yes . . . anything you say. I'll do anything . . .

Pastor: Hallelujah! *(He slaps* Mark *on the back and knocks him down. Immediately, all who were in the congregation jump up and say "Hallelujah" or "Praise the Lord" . . . it should be very exciting.* Mark *crawls on his hands and knees, through their legs, back to his original spot. The lights go out on the congregation and the music stops.)*

Mark *(picking himself up):* Whatever! *(Thinking)* But Jennifer isn't like that . . . she's more quiet.

(Lights come up on the opposite side of the stage and we see a congregation dressed in black, looking almost monklike with bad beards, women on one side . . . men on the other. They are very quiet. There is very soft, boring music playing in the background. This scene is completely the opposite of the other scene.)

Mark *(looks at the scene, then out to the audience):* They dress cool. *(He goes from his spot to join the scene. As he enters, every step he takes should be heard and magnified. Do this offstage on a microphone to make it sound like his shoes are squeaking. He stops and looks at his shoes then proceeds on. He starts to sit with the women, and we hear a giant gasp from the congregation as they all turn and stare at him. He quickly moves over to the men's side. As he gets there, they all kneel. He kneels too. Only when he does, we hear the bones in his knees creak. He bows his head and then starts to rub his nose as*

58

if he is going to sneeze. Everyone looks at him. The sneeze passes. Just as we think he is OK, he lets out a big sneeze and everyone in the congregation turns quickly and looks at him. There is a blackout.)

(Lights come immediately up on JENNIFER *and* SEAN *on the opposite side of the stage.)*

SEAN: I'll go get the car.

JENNIFER: I'll wait for Mark. Do you think he liked it?

SEAN: I don't know. I thought it was funny when Ben asked him to read the Bible and he called Psalms, Plasma. *(He laughs.)*

JENNIFER *(she looks at him with "it wasn't that funny" look):* Sean.

SEAN: It was funny. *(Beat)* I'll go get the car.

*(*JENNIFER *stands there awhile, then* MARK *enters.)*

JENNIFER: Sean went to get the car.

MARK: Cool. *(Under his breath he keeps repeating the word "Psalms.")*

JENNIFER: Are you all right?

MARK *(turning to her):* Psalms.

JENNIFER: Huh?

MARK: It's Psalms. I think I have it now.

JENNIFER *(she smiles):* I think I like Plasma better. *(There is a long pause as if they both don't know what to say.)*

MARK: I had a good time.

JENNIFER: Good.

MARK: I wasn't sure.

JENNIFER: We meet every Wednesday and Sunday.

MARK: I'm not sure I'm ready for Sundays. *(Long pause)* You . . . you really believe in this God stuff?

JENNIFER: Yeah, I do.

MARK: Cool.

JENNIFER: Do you?

MARK: I'm not sure. *(Beat)* Is that OK?

JENNIFER: Yeah.

MARK: How do you know . . . about God?

JENNIFER *(looks at him):* I just know. I . . . I guess it just seems more clear to believe than not to believe. I know that when I started to believe in Jesus, I just saw things differently. Something happened.

MARK *(pause):* I'll think about it.

JENNIFER: Here, take my Bible. Read some of it.

MARK: You sure?

JENNIFER: Sure.

(We hear a horn honk. They turn and look. JENNIFER and MARK start to leave. JENNIFER exits, but MARK turns and looks at the audience.)

MARK: It was . . . OK. Not how I pictured church. Everyone seemed cool. Sean was a little weird, but nobody called me . . . you know, evil or nothing. I . . . uh . . . I felt OK there.

(Lights come up on Mark's MOTHER. She is responding as if he has just asked her about "god.")

MOTHER: What do I think of God? Oh, my goodness, dear. That is a big subject. A BIG, BIG, BIG subject, like sex and where do babies come from. But you already know about that. *(Thinking)* Well, God is big. That is, if you believe in Him. You don't have to, you know. *(Thinking)* God. He is supposed to be everywhere *(beat),* although I'm not sure He hangs around your father. I don't know what to say about Him. Maybe you should ask someone else . . . your counselor. Yes, he would be a good one. Oh wait! Can you do that? I mean separation of church and state and all that. Can you do that? Well, ask him if you can ask him and if he says "yes," then just ask him. Your counselor . . . not God. Well, you could ask Him, too, if He exists. *(Beat)* How about a little fish with mango chutney?

(Lights go down on MOTHER and come up on the COUNSELOR, who is on the opposite side of the stage.)

COUNSELOR: God. Interesting question, Marion? Who is God? What is God? Do you believe in God? How do you feel about God? Think about it because it could be just a reaction to the need you feel for a father. And that is understandable, but we don't want any crutches. If you can embrace a higher power without falling into the trap of it being a crutch, then I say "go for it." God can be useful.

(Lights go down on the COUNSELOR and come up on MARK, who is center stage in a spotlight.)

MARK *(breaking a pencil):* Do you ever think there are too many "words"? I do. Just words . . . coming at you but not really meaning anything. I don't want God to be "useful" . . . like a can opener. Either He's real or He's not.

(Changing subjects) Hey, I was reading in the Bible that Jennifer let me use. There are these really great stories. Adam and Eve, ya know, how they lived in a garden until they screwed it up. Oh, and one that sort of "got" me. It was the story of Abraham. Not Abraham Lincoln . . . this dude named Abraham that was promised by God he would have a kid. Well, he got real old and still didn't have one, so his wife . . . uh, Sarah, told him to just have sex with her servant. Well, he did. Yeah. I mean, I don't blame him, but it was a stupid thing to do. Anyway, he had this son . . . Ishmael. Well, his wife got jealous, and it caused a major problem. Like that wasn't going to happen! And I thought my family was screwed up. Well, then he got his wife pregnant. Yeah, and he was like a hundred, and she was 90 or something. Pretty cool . . . *(reconsidering)* well, that she could still have a kid, not what she probably looked like. Not something you want to visualize, if you know what I mean. To cut this short, Abraham's wife told him the other son, Ishmael, and his mom, had to leave. And this it the part that got me. After they were thrown out and it looked like they were going to die, God talked to them and said "Hey, you're not going to die . . . I will make you a great nation . . . just as I promised." *(Pause)* Cool. Oh, I told my mom about all this . . . she just looked at me and said, "Broccoli?"

(A horn honks and lights come up on SEAN *and* JENNIFER *in the car.)*

JENNIFER: Why are you so quiet?

SEAN *(Long pause):* Is this going to be an every week event?

JENNIFER: What?

SEAN: Picking up Mark.

JENNIFER: He doesn't have a car.

SEAN: Maybe Jonathan can pick him up. He lives on this side of town.

JENNIFER: I didn't know it bugged you so much.

SEAN: Whatever.

*(*MARK *enters the scene and yells back.)*

MARK: I'll be back later. *(Getting into the car)* She thinks I'm getting too religious.

(Lights go down on the car and up on Mark's MOTHER.*)*

MOTHER: Well, dear . . . I just want you to be happy. That's all I want . . . you to be happy, happy, happy. If you think this religious stuff is where you can be happy, then I guess it's all right. I mean, you seem happy. Are you? Happy. It's just I don't understand some of these stories you're telling me. They seem so sexual and confusing. This man having sex with a slave and then with his wife. It's just not healthy . . . with all the disease out there. But you know all about that, right? If you're going to have sex, at least have

61

safe sex. That gentleman in the Bible should have considered that. And you know, Mark, that book seems a little violent too. Maybe they should make a Bible with a V chip. *(Beat)* Macaroni?

(The lights come up on a youth meeting. We see kids playing Ping-Pong, some sitting around talking, doing whatever you do in your youth "get together" times. MARK *walks into the scene, sits in a chair, and starts talking to* JENNIFER.*)*

MARK: Ishmael. He's like me.

JENNIFER: How?

MARK: His dad didn't want him . . . He just had a mom and they were out there all by themselves . . . but God took care of them. It's like me. Maybe God's been taking care of me and I didn't know it.

JENNIFER: Cool.

MARK *(handing her the Bible):* Anyway . . . thanks.

JENNIFER: No . . . you keep it. I can get another one.

MARK: But . . . you have stuff written all over it. I don't . . .

JENNIFER *(interrupting):* I want you to keep it. Besides, if you give a gift back, it's bad luck.

MARK: OK . . . but if you change your mind . . .

*(*SEAN *enters; he doesn't seem real happy.)*

SEAN: I think I'm going to leave early.

JENNIFER *(surprised):* Oh.

SEAN: Maybe you two can find a ride with somebody else. Ask Jonathan.

JENNIFER: Are you OK?

SEAN *(beat):* I'll talk to you later.

MARK: Hey . . . thanks for the . . .

SEAN *(interrupting and ignoring* MARK*):* See ya.

(He exits. JENNIFER *and* MARK *look at each other.)*

JENNIFER: I'll be back. *(She exits and moves to a spot on the other side of the stage where* SEAN *is standing. He is getting out his keys as if he is getting ready to get into his car.)* Sean, are you . . . ?

SEAN: What do you see in him?

JENNIFER: What?

SEAN: There must be something.

JENNIFER: Who are you talking about?

SEAN: Take a guess.

JENNIFER: Mark?

SEAN: Duh!

JENNIFER: Why are you getting so upset?

SEAN: He's a poser. He doesn't give a "jack" about God or the Bible or anything . . . he's just here because of you.

JENNIFER: So. *(Starting to get a little frustrated)* And you're wrong. He's asked a lot of questions.

SEAN: I bet he has. Has he asked you out?

JENNIFER: What if he has?

SEAN: Just answer my question.

(MARK *enters the scene and stands in the background.)*

JENNIFER: I don't have to answer anything.

SEAN: I thought we . . . *(catching himself)* . . . whatever. *(Starting to leave)*

JENNIFER: We what? We've gone out . . .

SEAN *(interrupting):* I don't like him.

JENNIFER: I thought he was a friend.

SEAN: You thought wrong. He doesn't fit in. None of the kids like him. He's a nerd, a geek, a loser.

JENNIFER: He is . . . *(She turns and* MARK *is standing there.)* Mark.

MARK *(he is obviously hurt, doesn't say anything, just drops the Bible into her hands and runs off.)*

JENNIFER *(she turns and looks at* SEAN*):* You're wrong . . . you're the loser. *(She exits.)* Mark.

(There is a blackout, then as each character speaks, a spot hits him or her. It remains on until this segment is done. This should be done very quickly. As one phrase is ending, the next one should start.)

COUNSELOR: You're a complicated young man.

FATHER: You're about as worthless as . . .

MOTHER: Just a confusing time.

FATHER: a four foot sack of . . .

JENNIFER: You're interesting.

FATHER: horse manure.

RONNIE: You're a loser.

SEAN: A poser.

COUNSELOR: I sense some anger.

RONNIE *(intimidating):* So, Batman . . . who invited you?

JENNIFER: You're interesting.

COUNSELOR: Alone.

SEAN: Nerd.

FATHER: You're about as worthless as a four foot sack of . . .

SEAN: Loser.

RONNIE *(mocking):* Bye, Marion.

COUNSELOR: Marion.

FATHER: horse manure.

RONNIE: Marion.

GROUP OF YOUNG KIDS *(mocking, singsong):* "Marion the Farion." *(This continues for some time.)*

FATHER: Marion.

COUNSELOR: Marion.

JENNIFER: It just seems more clear to believe than not to.

MOTHER: God?

JENNIFER: God.

COUNSELOR: We don't want any crutches.

MOTHER: If you believe in Him.

JENNIFER: It just seems more clear to believe than not to.

COUNSELOR: It could be just a reaction to the need you feel for a father.

FATHER: You're about as worthless as a four foot sack of horse manure.

MOTHER: The slimeball!

COUNSELOR: God can be useful.

JENNIFER: It just seems more clear to believe than not to.

MOTHER: That's big, big, big . . .

SEAN: None of the kids like him.

JENNIFER: Jesus.

RONNIE: Who invited you?

JENNIFER: Jesus.

MOTHER: If you believe in Him.

SEAN: Loser.

JENNIFER: He changed me.

COUNSELOR: God can be useful.

JENNIFER: Jesus. *(At this point, all the sounds stop, the kids stop taunting. There is a blackout on everyone except JENNIFER. There is a pause.)* Jesus.

(Lights come up onstage right. MARK is sitting there with his legs pulled up and his arms around them. His head is on his knees. JENNIFER enters.)

JENNIFER: You forgot something. *(She holds out the Bible to him.)*

(MARK just looks at her.)

JENNIFER: You can't give a gift back . . . it's bad luck.

MARK: Whatever.

JENNIFER: Sean's been hanging around Ronnie too much.

MARK *(reluctant)*: Yeah.

JENNIFER: Wanna let the air out of his tires?

(MARK smiles.)

JENNIFER: He didn't mean what he said.

MARK: Yes, he did.

JENNIFER *(pause)*: OK, maybe he did. But . . . he's just one person.

MARK: My whole life's full of "just one persons."

JENNIFER: He's not me.

MARK: And what makes you different?

JENNIFER *(pause)*: I don't know. Jesus.

MARK: Sean knows Jesus too. Right?

JENNIFER: Yeah . . . but he doesn't speak for Him.

MARK: He said I was a loser, a poser, nerd.

JENNIFER: You forgot "geek."

MARK (smiles): Geek. (Beat) Am I?

JENNIFER: Are you?

MARK: Asked you first.

JENNIFER: No. Are you?

MARK (thinks): Not a good time to ask.

JENNIFER: Ever since I met you . . . you seemed like you were someone . . . I don't know how to say this . . . (thinking) . . . you were someone wanting to belong but trying to show you didn't need anybody.

MARK: Yeah.

JENNIFER: We all need somebody, Mark.

MARK (pause): But it's hard to believe you belong . . . when everything around you says you don't belong . . . you don't matter.

JENNIFER: But you do. You do to me . . . you do to Jesus.

(MARK just looks at her.)

JENNIFER: We don't have to be the same. You're unique.

MARK (reminding her): Interesting.

JENNIFER: Yeah. So you're a little different . . . so was Jesus. So was Ishmael.

(MARK looks at her.)

JENNIFER: Just like you said. He was an outcast, his father didn't want him, but God still loved him and still gave him His promise.

MARK: And what promise has He given me?

JENNIFER: That you belong . . . to Him. And that will never change. OK?

MARK (looking at her and thinking): OK.

JENNIFER (she hands him the Bible): It's bad luck to give back a gift.

(MARK takes it and light goes to black. A spot comes up center stage and MARK walks into it.)

MARK: Being a teenager stinks . . . but I can handle it. I don't want to get all religious-sounding, but that night . . . I talked to God for the first time. I didn't hear a lot of words coming back at me . . . but I felt something in here *(touching his chest)* that told me . . . that told me . . . I belonged. *(He turns and looks to where the last scene took place, then back out to the audience.)* My name is Marion, as in Maid Marion, Kay as in K-A-Y, my parents wanted a girl, and Riddle as in a joke or a confusing puzzle . . . *(he stops himself)* with a very, very surprising end.

(Light goes to black.)

PERFORMANCE
LICENSING AGREEMENT

Lillenas Publishing Resources
Performance Licensing
P.O. Box 419527, Kansas City, MO 64141

Name _____

Organization _____

Address _____

City_____ State _____ ZIP_____

Circle the play being performed:

Play_____ **FIFTH HOUR** by Jerry Cohagan _____

or

_____ **BEFORE CLASS AND AFTER** by Bob Hoose _____

or

_____ **JUST CALL ME MARK** by Jim Custer _____

Number of performances intended _____

Approximate dates _____

Amount remitted* $_____

Mail to Lillenas at the address above.

Order performance copies of this script from your local bookstore or directly from the publisher 1-800-877-0700.

*$15.00 for the first performance; $10.00 each subsequent performance. Payable U.S. funds.

PERFORMANCE
LICENSING AGREEMENT

Lillenas Publishing Resources
Performance Licensing
P.O. Box 419527, Kansas City, MO 64141

Name _____

Organization _____

Address _____

City _____ State _____ ZIP _____

Circle the play being performed:

Play_____ **FIFTH HOUR** by Jerry Cohagan _____

or

_____ **BEFORE CLASS AND AFTER** by Bob Hoose _____

or

_____ **JUST CALL ME MARK** by Jim Custer _____

Number of performances intended _____

Approximate dates _____

Amount remitted* $ _____

Mail to Lillenas at the address above.

Order performance copies of this script from your local bookstore or directly from the publisher 1-800-877-0700.

*$15.00 for the first performance; $10.00 each subsequent performance. Payable U.S. funds.